How To Manage Money

Methods For Developing Independent Skills In Money
Management: Participating In Practical Lessons
And Activities To Foster Confidence, Problem-solving
Abilities, And Skill Growth

Konrad Fichtinger

TABLE OF CONTENT

Health Insurance

This represents the culmination of the three sequential steps that necessitate careful consideration prior to embarking on any investment venture.

Houses and cars tend to be among the most expensive purchases one is likely to make.

Education and medical expenses typically account for the largest portion of expenditures.

Regardless of your preferences, it is possible that a member of your family may encounter medical expenses. It is uncertain how much that can accrue to. However, the decision lies with you today regarding the choice between personally covering the costs or seeking coverage through your Health Insurance.

Do not allow a single health condition to deplete your entire financial resources.

Once again, it is important to note that insurance serves as an expenditure and should not be seen as an avenue for wealth accumulation. It serves only as a precaution against a forthcoming, considerably larger financial burden. Naturally, our desire is for none of our medical insurance premiums to be rendered ineffective.

If you believe that health insurance is currently unnecessary due to your youthful and robust condition, reconsider your standpoint. Health insurance additionally provides coverage for injuries resulting from accidents. Illnesses such as dengue fever, foodborne illnesses, and so forth. Furthermore, it has the potential to affect individuals regardless of their state of health.

During one's early years, it is feasible (though unadvisable) to depend on the insurance coverage offered by one's employer. Peruse the intricacies of the coverage limit, inclusions, exclusions, and other pertinent details. carefully.

Let us now explore methods of determining the most suitable health insurance plan for your needs. Arguably, the primary challenge associated with the majority of finance topics lies in the seemingly inexhaustible array of options at hand.

There are myriad aspects that should be taken into consideration when examining your health insurance policy. While the majority of individuals request all, you have the option to select whether you desire the entirety.

Family Floater policies are a prudent choice for conjugal partnerships. Individual premiums are comparatively reduced, alongside an overall improvement in coverage. However, a downside of family plans lies in the limited options available when two members of the same family experience illnesses within a year. This is due to the fact that the aggregate sum to be paid by the insurance company remains constant.

This is the reason why the inclusion of multiple restorations of the sum assured is an exceptional attribute. Regardless of prior utilization during the year, your sum assured will be reinstated.

One crucial matter that must be attended to is the maximum age at which the policy can be renewed. It is likely that medical costs will rise as one's age advances. It will become essential for one to maintain coverage during their elderly years, particularly after retirement.

The daily room charge sub-limit can significantly deplete your financial resources. An example is required to illustrate this. Allow me to propose that the maximum limit for your daily room charge is set at Rs6,000/-. Due to the scarce availability or any other underlying circumstances, you opt for a room with a daily rate of Rs10,000/-. Here, you will have the right to assert a reimbursement of only 60% of your TOTAL expenses. Not merely limited to the cost of renting the room. Should the doctor's fee amount to Rs50,000/- during your stay, it will ultimately result in the insurance company paying a sum of only Rs30,000/-, despite that. This remains independent of the overall coverage provided by your policy.

Opt for a policy that permits elevated daily room rates. Preferably, a situation where private room availability is guaranteed without any limits on room rental fees.

Please ensure that the company maintains a network of hospitals across the country, particularly in your locality. Please take into consideration that this list may undergo frequent modifications.

The full range of diseases should be encompassed by the entirety of the cover. Several measures impose limitations on the coverage of each individual ailment.

Choose pre- and post-hospitalization care. This will encompass the prospective diagnostic examinations prior to hospitalization, as well as necessary medications, and other related items. afterwards.

Authorization should be completed within a maximum time frame of one hour.

It is imperative to incorporate day-care treatments.

The insurance policy should include provisions for in-home treatment as an alternative to hospitalization in the event that it is not feasible due to any circumstances.

The policy ought to cover expenses related to non-consumable items. This encompasses the expenses associated with sanitizing agents, facial coverings, protective hand gear, cotton materials, and other disposable items utilized during the course of your medical care.

The inclusion of an annual health check-up confers an additional benefit.

Alternative therapies such as Naturopathy and Ayurveda, among others. Should you intend to utilize any similar service. It is important to be aware that Ayush centres are insuranced by a limited number of insurers.

I would consistently opt for cashless claims, as it alleviates the inconvenience of making payment upfront and subsequently requesting reimbursement from the insurer. For non-cashless claims, it is imperative to consistently maintain the necessary funds to make upfront payments.

Consider add-on factors like:

The accident coverage entails a predetermined compensation based on the nature and severity of your sustained injury.

Disability insurance, providing you with a predetermined and substantial sum upon diagnosis of a severe medical condition. You are not required to provide any supporting documentation in this instance.

If you are currently in that particular phase of life, it would be prudent to contemplate securing Maternity cover. With the inclusion of riders such as this one, the insurer can reasonably anticipate that you will likely make use of the benefits you have chosen to incorporate. As a means of recompense, they typically opt to raise the premium. Ensure that you refrain from incurring costs that exceed what would have been expended during your hospitalization.

Tip:

Mind the exclusions.

Please ensure to consider the following factors in a conscientious manner: 1) Examine the limitations or restrictions on coverage. 2) Evaluate the co-payment requirements. 3) Take into account the presence of any loadings, if applicable. 4) Assess the deductibles that might obligate you to cover a specific percentage of each claim. The policy ought not to include any of these.

Exercise greater discernment in regards to the aspects the insurance provider has chosen to exclude from the policy, in contrast to the elements they have decided to include.

Postscript: In the event that the policy specifies a room category such as "single private room," it could potentially provide coverage for the most economical option available within that category at the hospital.

Kindly remember to avail the deduction provided under Section 80D when submitting your Income Tax Return.

An excellent enhancement option for your health insurance coverage is a premium-level top-up. It provides coverage for your medical expenses, although not in their entirety. You are required to pay a deductible, which constitutes the initial charges.

It is customary to obtain a super top-up coverage exceeding the sum assured of your primary insurance policy. Through the combination of both elements, a substantial extent of coverage is achieved.

For instance, suppose that your foundational policy provides coverage for medical expenses of up to Rs. Ten Lakh. It would be advisable to consider acquiring an additional coverage of Rs. Fifty Lakh, with a deductible of Rs. Ten Lakh. As per the terms outlined, the primary policy in your bill will provide coverage for up to ten lakh, while the supplementary top-up will assume responsibility for any expenses exceeding this amount, up to a maximum of fifty lakh.

Super top-ups offer a more cost-effective alternative to base policies due to the inclusion of deductibles.

It is strongly advised that you obtain this additional coverage in addition to your primary policy.

With that being said, it is essential for you to distinguish between opting for a solitary extensive coverage and opting for a super top-up.

1) The base policy and the super top-up policy are distinct and autonomous policies. To acquire both, it will be necessary for you to submit two distinct claims. This situation is further compounded when the policies you possess originate from two distinct companies. Particularly so if the affiliated healthcare providers of both organizations are distinct. Therefore, endeavor to obtain your fundamental policy and premium coverage from the identical provider on the corresponding date.

2) Super top-up policies do not provide any restoration benefits or No Claim Bonus.

In summary, approach both policies as distinct entities, and inquire about all essential aspects of each one. For instance, inquire about aspects such as the duration of the waiting period, the maximum limit on room rent, and so forth.

After the acquisition of health insurance, it is advisable to conduct oneself as if one were uninsured. Please ensure you prioritize your wellbeing.

Simply contact an insurance consultant or utilize an online comparison platform to fulfill your needs. Kindly communicate your desired policy features explicitly and inquire about any exclusions that may be present. Simple.

In the event of possessing undisclosed insurance coverage, be it life or health-related, the absence of knowledge regarding such policies within your family renders them practically ineffective.

It would be of no advantage to you or your family if they remain unaware of the existence of a claimable item. Create a journal or employ a password-secured Word/Excel document to record all your financial transactions. It is imperative for your family to possess knowledge regarding your insurances and investments in order to avail themselves of the associated benefits.

Categorization of Present Assets and Present Liabilities

Working capital, along with the gap between current assets and current liabilities, is employed as a basis for calculating permissible bank finance.

Current Asset Includes

Cash and cash equivalents refer to monetary holdings or investments with high liquidity, capable of being readily converted into cash if they are not already in a liquid state.

Outstanding liabilities: Monetary amounts owed to a company by individuals or entities.

Inventory: The valuation of accessible commodities procured yet not yet disposed of, in addition to unredeemed stock.

Immediate investment options encompass various financial instruments, such as money markets, savings accounts, treasury bills, and government bonds.

Accounts receivable: Typically found within the current assets section of the balance sheet, accounts receivable pertains to any outstanding amounts owed to the company and is classified as such if the repayment period is expected to be completed within one year. More precisely, a note receivable can be defined as a documented undertaking to receive a sum of money on a designated future date. Typically, the funds comprise of both the interest and principal amounts.

Prepaid expenditures: Insurance premiums that are still outstanding and have not yet reached their expiration date.

Investments with liquidity: Equities, fixed-income securities, and other financial instruments

"In particular, it encompasses the following components:

Financial Resources: Cash and Deposits

Governamental and trust securities investments" and "Bank fixed deposits

Trade receivables originating from Sales apart from deferred receivables.

Deferred receivables to be paid in installments within a period of one year

Primary resources and constituent elements utilized in the course of the production process

Equities within the progression encompassing intermediary products

"Concluded merchandise, encompassing items currently in transit.

Other consumable spares

Prepayment of taxes

Prepaid expenses.

Progress in acquiring raw materials, components, and consumable supplies.

Funds will be received from the sale of contracted fixed assets within the upcoming 12-month period.

Current Liabilities includes

Outstanding liabilities: The sum owed by a business for goods or services obtained on credit, without the issuance of a formal promissory note.

Accounts payable: The monetary obligation owed by a company to its suppliers for the goods received from them in the normal course of business operations.

Bonds payable refer to the total principal value of the bonds issued by a company that remain outstanding and have not reached maturity as of the date recorded on the balance sheet.

Outstanding loan balance: The principal amount that remains to be repaid on a contractual agreement, such as a loan obtained from a financial institution.

Accounts payable for employee wages: The outstanding liabilities for hours worked by employees but not yet remunerated as of the balance sheet date.

Accrued salaries: The sum of wages or salaries that have been incurred by a company's workforce, but have not yet been disbursed by the company.

Amount of income taxes owed to the federal, state, and local governments and currently payable

Accrued interest: The outstanding amount of interest that the company is liable for on the date of the balance sheet

Other outstanding liabilities: Formal financial obligations that have been contracted by the company but have not yet been documented in the accounts payable records.

Accrued revenues and advance payments from customers

Inclusive of thorough information, it encompasses

Short-term Borrowings

Unsecured Loans

Short-term public deposit reaching its maturity date within a twelve-month period

Various creditors for the procurement of raw materials and expendable inventory, as well as spare parts.

Accrued interest and additional charges not yet payable.

Prepayments received from clients

Deposits originating from dealer entities, selling agents, and other related parties.

Payments of term loans, debentures, deferred payment credits, redeemable preference shares, and long-term deposits that are due within a period of one year.

Legal obligations, encompassing sales tax, excise duty, outstanding provident fund contributions, tax provisions, and liabilities arising from statutory dues.

Miscellaneous current liabilities include the following: a) Dividends, liabilities associated with expenses, gratuity payable within a one-year period, other provisions, and any other outstanding payments due within twelve months.

Balance sheet Analysis

Balance sheet analysis entails the comprehensive examination of a company's assets, liabilities, and equities. The analysis dissects a complicated collection of data and statistics into easily understandable and comparable elements. The examination of a comprehensive collection of financial statements is an integral part of conducting a balance sheet analysis. The statements presented adhere to the following principles.

a) Financial statements for buying and producing goods

b) Income statement

c) Financial statement "d) Statement of financial position "e) Consolidated balance sheet "f) Financial report "g) Accounting statement of balance "h) Financial statement of accounts "i) Statement of financial condition "j) Statement of assets and liabilities

"d) Report by the auditor

e) Report from the Board of Directors

f) Orders for the assessment of Income Tax and Goods and Services Tax (GST)

By conducting an analysis of a company's financial data, one can ascertain:

The extent to which the firm's liabilities exceed its shareholders' equity.

The prompt requests an alternative phrase that maintains a formal tone, expressing the concept of the speed at which customers are settling their invoices. Here's a suggestion: "The promptness with which customers are fulfilling their payment obligations."

Whether there is a decrease or an increase in short-term cash.

The proportion of tangible assets and the extent to which they are derived from accounting transactions.

Whether products are experiencing a higher rate of return compared to the industry norm

It is now time to liquidate the existing inventory.

Whether the allocation of resources towards research and development is yielding favorable outcomes

Whether the interest coverage ratio pertaining to the bonds is experiencing an upward or downward trend.

The mean rate of interest being paid by a company on its debt.

The allocation of profits toward expenditure or reinvestment within the organization.

Report of Auditor

The inclusion of the auditor's report as an integral component of the Balance sheet is of paramount importance in conducting a comprehensive examination of the financial statements. Financial statements are compiled with the objective of ascertaining the financial status of the organization, which holds significant relevance for prospective and current shareholders, suppliers, staff members, debtors, lenders, patrons, financiers, governmental entities, and other stakeholders.

Each and every company is liable to undergo an audit. Auditors take record of the company with respect to its current state of affairs. The appended comments accompanying the financial statements include analysis of the balance sheet, profit and loss account, and other pertinent documents. The auditors further communicate any departure from widely recognized accounting principles. The note illustrates the contested statutory obligations including Income Tax, Sales Tax, Custom duty, and so on. The note also includes information about any instances of default in fulfilling its debt obligation, along with the underlying cause. The report indicates whether sufficient allocation has been made for depreciation, taxation, and dividend disbursement. It encompasses crucial information for all parties involved.

Saving Around the House

Each and every one of us has experienced the same situation. On occasion, the quantity of available funds may be slightly less than what one is accustomed to, necessitating the implementation of noteworthy alterations in one's lifestyle to maintain financial stability. This may be attributed to the holiday season, an unforeseen alteration in one's professional trajectory, or being burdened with an unanticipated financial obligation. Fortunately, there are numerous effortless approaches to reduce your expenses at present without enduring significant discomfort caused by the inconvenient financial pressure.

• Design a menu and adhere to it.

One effective approach to mitigate the gradual depletion of funds in your bank account is to ensure that you arrive at the grocery store equipped with a meticulously planned list outlining both the specific items you intend to purchase and the schedule for consuming them.

Research indicates that American households squander a substantial amount of money annually on food. The layout of grocery stores is strategically designed to entice impulsive buying. By refraining from wandering through sections that do not align with your predetermined shopping list, you are likely to yield substantial savings when it comes time to settle the bill. Moreover, adhering to this principle will also spare you from having to discard unused or expired items from your refrigerator at a later point in time. Furthermore, as a result of prearranged family meals, you will be relieved of the arduous responsibility of determining the evening's menu.

• Disconnect all devices that are not in use.

How often do you utilize the can opener or blender, as a matter of fact? maybe once a week? Inspect the electrical outlets throughout your residence to identify any unnecessary devices that remain plugged in. Indeed, even the power adapter for your mobile device. You may observe a moderate decline solely in your upcoming utility statement, yet it could yield a marginal impact (while also decreasing your carbon footprint to a lesser extent).

• Use coupons.

Make the most of the discounted opportunities offered by retailers without exceeding reasonable limits. In numerous contemporary supermarkets, patrons now have the option to digitally transfer coupons onto their customer loyalty cards, thereby eliminating the requirement for a physical coupon to avail instant price reductions.

• Prepare a midday meal in advance to bring to your place of employment.

Whilst it is conceivable that your mornings and daytimes are already filled with various obligations, taking the time to prepare a packed lunch for either school or work could potentially result in significant financial savings. Furthermore, it has the potential to offer an additional source of motivation to sustain a nourishing dietary regimen. By establishing an effective schedule, such as preparing packed lunches in the evening to be refrigerated overnight or prepping meals during the weekend for the upcoming work week, it is highly probable that opting for a homemade lunch will prove to be a more economically viable and nutritionally beneficial choice compared to dining at restaurants.

• Prepare your own coffee. • Brew your own coffee. • Produce your own coffee. • Brew a pot of coffee yourself. • Prepare a cup of coffee independently.

Despite the delightful taste of those warm caramel macchiatos and iced lattes, the price per unit is considerably higher compared to the amount you would spend on making your own beverage at home prior to departing. Acquire a sizeable thermal travel mug capable of sustaining you throughout the entire morning, subsequently avoid the services of a barista and allow the coffeemaker to brew your coffee instead. The potential financial benefits to your pocketbook are significant.

• Participate in complimentary local community gatherings.

Whilst engaging in activities such as attending movies, concerts, and dining out can be enjoyable, it is important to acknowledge that they often come with a substantial cost attached. If you are a resident of a city that hosts public events, we recommend giving them a chance. There might be additional factors that you may not have considered, and it is probable that investing in extracurricular activities would be more favorable compared to availing oneself of the town's complimentary attractions.

• Visit a library. • Explore a library. • Pay a visit to a library. • Utilize the resources of a library. • Engage with the collections at a library.

Should you be inclined to extend an opportunity, your nearby libraries offer an abundance of extraordinary resources. Not only do they possess an extensive assortment of books that can be readily and freely accessed for reading, but they may also possess a curated compilation of music and movies that align with your preferences, offered free of cost. Furthermore, a noteworthy aspect of these establishments is their provision of family-oriented activities, which are entirely devoid of any charges.

• Consume more produce.

Being a consumer of meat or even a consumer of both meat and plants may lead to a slightly elevated expenditure on food, in comparison to individuals adhering to a diet based solely on plants. Why? Indeed, meat does come at a high price. Decreasing your consumption of meat can yield substantial savings on your grocery expenses, in addition to offering various benefits such as heightened vitamin intake from fruits and vegetables.

• Remunerate for purchases using legal tender.

It may appear uncomplicated, and indeed it is. Using a credit card tends to diminish the mindfulness of spending and create an illusion of money being more detached from reality. Conversely, opting for cash as your preferred payment method encourages a pause for reflection, prompting a more conscious evaluation of the exact amounts being expended during each transaction. When you opt to utilize the paper instead of the plastic during the transaction, you may pleasantly discover that your spending becomes more conservative.

• Furnish children with artistic activities.

There exist numerous strategies for ensuring the engagement and contentment of young individuals while adhering to financial constraints, despite the often exorbitant costs associated with children's toys and activities. Even a rudimentary artistic endeavor, such as constructing a knick knack box using wooden popsicle sticks and adhesive substances, can offer ample amusement, stimulate mental acuity, and bestow a sense of gratification upon the children involved. Additionally, it will present you with a cost-effective opportunity to enjoy valuable moments of familial bonding.

• Adjust the temperature during your absence. • Modify the temperature while you are not present. • Adapt the temperature while you are not in the vicinity. • Make alterations to the temperature in your absence.

It is highly likely that your electricity bill will surge significantly during periods of extreme cold or heat due to the increased usage of air conditioning and heating systems. However, by making slight adjustments to the thermostat when you are away from home, such as increasing or decreasing the temperature by a few degrees depending on the season, and returning it to its original setting upon your arrival in the evening, you may potentially mitigate the extent of the issue. You can trust that the energy conserved during your periods of rest will accumulate effectively.

Budgeting Tools

The majority of individuals have made attempts at budgeting, however, the execution phase often presents itself as one of the most daunting aspects. Regardless of the level of detail in your budget, its effectiveness will be undermined if you are unable to adhere to its guidelines, rendering all your budgeting efforts inconsequential. You will require resources that enable you to adhere to your budget; otherwise, you are likely to abandon your efforts prematurely. May I inquire about the specific instruments under discussion? Presented below are a selection of them:

Envelope System

If you are a beginner or have encountered limited success with budgeting and struggle to adhere to the budget, the envelope system is unquestionably your optimal choice. In this approach, individuals classify their expenses into distinct categories such as transportation, sustenance, charitable contributions, savings, among others, and subsequently locate envelopes to designate each expenditure type. For the aforementioned categories, it is recommended that you procure distinct envelopes, clearly labeled as food, transportation, charitable donations, savings, and so forth.

Whenever one intends to incur an expenditure concerning sustenance, one should withdraw funds from the designated envelope allocated for food expenses. If you desire to allocate funds for transportation expenses, kindly extract cash from the designated envelope labeled 'transportation'. In order to facilitate the successful execution of this plan, it is crucial to utilize the aforementioned expenditure tracker to generate an approximation of your expenditures for various items, thus enabling you to allocate the appropriate amount of money to each envelope. If insufficient funds remain in a particular envelope, it is essential to cease expenditures within that category. It is imperative not to transfer funds from alternate envelopes, as doing so would undermine the efficacy of the system. This holds especially true in cases where that particular category is something you can easily forego. This can serve as an effective means of preventing excessive spending.

Leverage Technology

In this era characterized by technological advancements, it would be regrettable for one to not employ any of the accessible mechanisms that have transformed this period into a technological epoch. Nonetheless, you can acquire proficiency in utilizing certain budgeting utilities.

Mint.com

This particular product happens to be highly favored by many individuals and serves to enhance individuals' lives, especially for those who are embarking on their journey of budgeting. The site's appeal lies in its ability to establish connections with all your accounts, providing you with comprehensive knowledge of your expenditure. It integrates savings accounts, checking accounts, credit cards, and various expenditures into a single platform, further enhancing the user experience by facilitating the establishment of monthly budgets and financial objectives. We offer a feature that enables the delivery of bill reminders directly to your mobile device, along with alerts notifying you as you approach your specified spending limit for a designated interval. That appears to be a streamlined approach to budgeting.

Money Strands

This represents another cost-free, user-friendly budgeting tool that presents appealing services. MoneyStrands has a greater inclination towards financial planning as opposed to mere transaction tracking. The tool is equipped with bar graphs, calendars, and other visual aids that facilitate the tracking of bill payments and expenses.

In addition to connecting to your accounts for expense tracking purposes, it goes a step further by generating personalized budgets tailored to your specific spending patterns. In light of the available data concerning your expenses, the platform additionally provides you with individually customized financial advice. It compels you to embrace the practice of budgeting wholeheartedly.

Budget Tracker

The nomenclature of this tool is seemingly evident. It possesses a distinct capability of tracking transactions, regardless of whether or not you provide your confidential bank login details. It has the capability to tailor on-site applications, thereby enhancing the tool's ability to monitor a wider range of items. Subsequently, it presents you with the option of selecting the desired information to be showcased in an order progressing from the broad to the precise. Similar to the way MoneyStrands operates, the graphs and calendars on the website will display the tracking outcomes for your account.

If you opt to synchronize accounts, it should be noted that BudgetTracker has a drawback in that the synchronization is not instantaneous.

Budget Simple

For individuals seeking a financial management solution primarily for the purpose of monitoring expenses and organizing bills, BudgetSimple could serve as an apt choice. The name can be easily pronounced and the user experience is straightforward. It represents one of the most straightforward methods to establish your budget. It facilitates the evaluation of your budgetary advancement, and given that one of its primary objectives is to facilitate debt-free status, it guarantees financial headway.

My Spending Plan

If you are an individual who favors the practice of safeguarding financial resources by allocating them to designated envelopes and conducting transactions exclusively with physical currency, with the explicit goal of visualizing the expenditure and remaining balance within each envelope, then you will undoubtedly find great appeal in My Spending Plan. This tool aids in the development of a budget, thereby facilitating adherence to one's financial resources through implementation of the envelope system. The envelope system entails allocating designated funds for various purposes, which can be segregated into labeled envelopes, denoting the intended amount and specific allocation of the funds. In addition, My Spending Plan also provides you with notifications regarding upcoming account obligations and any outstanding payments that require prompt attention. The proposal is intended to facilitate the establishment of a lifestyle that aligns with your financial resources. Additionally, it offers an effective means of facilitating progress towards one's financial objectives through the provision of promotions and coupons.

The aforementioned list is not comprehensive, as there exist numerous additional tools that provide varying functionalities, some of which may exhibit certain resemblances. Their approach empowers you to evaluate and select the most suitable option, putting you in control of the decision-making process. Your decision has the potential to establish a lifelong or, at the very least, a enduring friendship.

How To Enhance Financial Acumen

Acquiring proficient personal finance skills is highly advantageous as they enable individuals to effectively manage their finances, allocate funds for retirement planning, and establish a contingency reserve. These are the skills that are not imparted to young children by either parents or educational institutions. Nevertheless, these competencies are indispensable in the long term.

Are you aware of whether you possess characteristics of being a spender or a saver? What are the most effective strategies for managing finances and achieving financial well-being?

Outlined below are the fundamental steps for developing and enhancing your financial aptitude, eliminating the necessity of seeking guidance from a professional financial advisor.

Know the Flow.

The initial step entails determining your monthly cash flow. It is crucial to comprehend the precise sum of money at your disposal on a monthly basis. Despite the potential challenges associated with the task, there exists a multitude of online applications that can prove to be advantageous.

You have the option to select the most appropriate personal finance software and complimentary online budgeting tools to assess your monthly cash flow and acquire supplementary insights into your existing financial standing. This will serve as the foundation for the cultivation and enhancement of your financial aptitude. In what other manner might you ascertain whether you possess a proclivity for expenditure or conservation?

Based on the most recent survey undertaken by CNBC and Acorns, in collaboration with SurveyMonkey, a significant majority, specifically 56%, of the American populace identifies as savers, prioritizing savings over expenditures. Approximately three-quarters (75%) of individuals attempt to manage their own finances, whereas only a minority of individuals (17%) seek the assistance of a financial planner to aid in their money management endeavors.

Jon Cohen, the research officer at SurveyMonkey, stated that the findings of this survey demonstrate that the prevailing sentiment among Americans is a strong sense of confidence with regards to their saving capabilities. Nevertheless, this remains a significant issue concerning individuals' personal finances, necessitating the impartation of financial literacy to enhance money management skills.

Create a Budget.

Numerous individuals hold the viewpoint that crafting a budget is not a fundamental requirement, disregarding its potential to mitigate a multitude of financial errors. Failure to adhere to this crucial step and persisting in maintaining your former lifestyle will indefinitely impede your ability to attain financial independence. Every expenditure category in your monthly budget requires a specific amount of funds. Implementing a budget enables individuals to proactively determine the precise allocation of funds for each expenditure category, thereby ensuring financial stability until the subsequent income cycle.

Once you acquire a comprehensive understanding of your expenditure patterns, you will be better equipped to make prudent choices concerning the potential elimination or reduction of certain expense categories. When devising your budget, you have the option of utilizing a budgeting spreadsheet or simply enumerating the subsequent categories:

Invest Money Consciously.

I regret not being able to impart upon my younger self the importance of cultivating the practice of saving or investing. According to Robert Pagliarini, an esteemed personal financial advisor, initiating this habit is relatively effortless, even with the initial accumulation of a few dollars per week.

Investment involves the process of capital appreciation. This may serve as an additional means of accumulating funds for retirement or unexpected financial needs. Moreover, this particular method represents one of the most advantageous approaches for remaining on course amidst perpetual inflation and achieving an elevated rate of return.

Take into consideration the cultivation of this skill and exercise prudence in allocating your financial resources. Please bear in mind that you are a valuable resource that requires investment in your education, skills, and other areas. Consider exploring specialized certifications, academic programs, or web-based courses in personal development that have the potential to yield valuable returns on investment with a modest financial commitment at present.

Become a Wise Consumer.

Is it your regular practice to compile a list of groceries required prior to visiting a supermarket? Do you consistently engage in the pursuit of securing the most favorable pricing? Have you ever availed yourself of coupons or perused discounted offers?

Furthermore, there exists a wide array of valuable applications and software that can effectively inform you about exclusive promotions and present-day discount vouchers, thereby enhancing your purchasing habits and enabling you to conserve monetary resources.

Initiate the process of meticulously tracking all expenditures made. Indeed, albeit the endeavor of scouring for optimal prices, formulating comprehensive shopping lists, and perusing supermarket prices prior to making purchases demands considerable time and exertion, the rewards derived from this diligence are immeasurable. Endeavor to incorporate this skill into your daily life, and you will observe a noticeable impact on the financial resources that will be conserved.

2.3.2 Current accounts

Checking accounts yield nearly as poor a return on investment as physical currency over an extended period of time. The sole disparity lies in the minimal interest rate they could potentially provide.

Additionally, they have the ability to mitigate the risk of loss, theft, fire, and other related perils. However, the deleterious effects of inflation still erode their worth in a similar manner.

Over the course of the extended period, current accounts also contribute to financial deterioration as a result of the erosion of purchasing power brought about by inflation.

Its primary utilization is to circumvent the retention of the entirety of the funds designated for expenditure in physical currency denominations. Furthermore, they prove to be highly beneficial for facilitating direct debits of bills, credit card payments, and transfers, among various other transactions.

All the operations I have discussed pertain to expenditures, and this correlation is not fortuitous. Due to the nature of current accounts, they are exclusively designated for funds allocated towards regular and immediate expenses. Funds allocated for savings or investment should not be retained within a current account.

Certain present-day bank accounts offer an interest rate marginally exceeding zero. Despite this possibility, it is highly improbable that the interest rate would exceed inflation for a substantial portion of an individual's lifetime, with a likelihood of 99.99%. Consequently, our purchasing power would consistently diminish with each passing day.

If a significant economic catastrophe were to occur such as armed conflicts, excessive inflation, or the complete breakdown of a financial system, the funds held in current accounts would be subject to the same outcome as physical currency in the form of banknotes and coins.

2.3.3 Accounts that accrue interest and deposits with fixed tenures

They represent the subsequent progression beyond regular checking accounts.

The primary distinction associated with current accounts lies in the fact that interest-bearing accounts and fixed-term deposits offer interest rates typically equivalent to the prevailing inflation rate. Occasionally, the figure exceeds the inflation rate marginally, while at other times, it falls slightly below it.

Fixed-term deposits typically offer a marginally higher interest rate compared to interest-bearing accounts, as this serves as a means of offsetting the inherent drawback of limited liquidity that these types of deposits entail.

As a generalization, interest-bearing accounts tend to yield slightly less than inflation, and longer-term deposits tend to yield slightly more than inflation. Nevertheless, there are instances wherein these generalizations prove untrue.

If the remuneration were equal, it would be illogical to allocate your funds to a fixed-term deposit, as the sacrifice of liquidity would be futile unless an impending decrease in interest rates is anticipated. Ultimately, in the event that this occurs, it is likely that interest-bearing accounts will yield a diminished return in a relatively brief period. On the other hand, deposits are obliged to remit the predetermined sum throughout the entirety of the deposit term, irrespective of any fluctuations in the prevailing interest rates during the course of the deposit. Given the circumstances, it would be prudent to consider initiating a term deposit as a means to secure a consistent yield over an extended duration, as interest-bearing accounts have the propensity to alter their offered returns at their discretion, often without prior notice.

The selection between interest-bearing accounts and term deposits is contingent upon the prevailing interest rate associated with each financial instrument, in addition to considerations concerning liquidity. Both are important. There is typically minimal disparity observed in interest rates between remunerated accounts and deposits. Therefore, in the scenario of funds designated for investment in the stock market, I opine that prioritizing liquidity is essential. It is more advantageous to have immediate access to the funds rather than having to endure a waiting period until the deposit matures, thus enabling timely investment. During the duration of the waiting period, there may arise an opportunity cost that surpasses the marginal increase in profitability provided by the deposit. Investment decisions, such as the purchase of shares, should not be contingent upon the maturity date of a deposit.

Interest-bearing accounts and fixed-term deposits represent the minimum requirements for funds designated for investment purposes that should be deemed acceptable. Funds designated for investment purposes must not be held in physical currency or non-interest-bearing current accounts.

Long-term investments that yield interest are not optimal, but in the short term, they serve as an advantageous avenue to maintain liquidity and generate modest returns while avoiding the potential drawbacks of temporary market fluctuations.

Interest-bearing accounts and fixed-term deposits may not be ideal for long-term investments due to the significant erosion of their purchasing power caused by inflation, which is the crucial factor to consider.

Setting Your Goals

Establishing objectives involves developing a strategic blueprint that motivates and guides individuals or a collective towards reaching that objective. In contrast to mere desires and impulsive intentions, goals possess a greater degree of purposeful intent. Establishing objectives involves guiding one's cognitive, emotional, and behavioral processes towards attaining the desired outcome. Through the implementation of this strategy, the individual responsible for setting goals establishes an envisioned outcome that deviates from their present circumstances, thus generating a discrepancy that spurs subsequent endeavors. Parameters for goal-setting, such as the SMART criteria, can serve as a compass to steer the process of goal establishment.

Within the realm of scholarly literature pertaining to management and personal development, the establishment of objectives occupies a principal position. Significantly, research conducted by Edwin A." Locke and his colleagues have effectively displayed that setting more demanding and aspirational objectives yields a higher magnitude of performance enhancement in comparison to setting simplistic or broad goals. The objectives need to be meticulously defined, adhering to specific timeframes, and present a level of difficulty that compels effort. Vague objectives consume the restricted cognitive capacity available. Pragmatically, setting excessively compressed timelines exacerbates the challenges associated with the desired objective beyond original intentions, and imbalanced deadlines lack the necessary impetus.

It would be advantageous to establish ambitious objectives that lie within the 90th percentile of performance, provided that the hindrance to attaining such a level of performance is primarily attributed to motivation rather than ability. The presence of impartial acceptance, capacity to attain the objective, and the lack of conflicting objectives collectively aid in establishing a constructive correlation between the level of goal complexity and task accomplishment.

Based on the concept proposed by Locke et al., the presence of varied performance objectives serves as the fundamental and uncomplicated motivational factor underlying the superior performance of certain individuals in comparison to others.

"The fundamental concept within the theory is:

1. Establishing challenging and specific objectives proves significantly more efficacious than establishing simplistic goals, having no goals at all, or even setting an abstract objective such as fostering a culture of excellence among others.

2. Under the conditions of maintaining a consistent level of ability and assuming the presence of commitment to the goal, an escalation in goal level leads to an improvement in performance.

3. The impact of factors such as commendation, evaluation, or individual participation in determining goals is limited to the extent that they foster individuals' selection and subsequent dedication to a specific challenging objective.

History

In the year 1935, the inaugural empirical investigation was carried out by Cecil Alec Mace.

In the midst of the 1960s, Edwin A. Locke embarked upon an inquiry into the establishment of goals. He dedicated over three decades of his life to researching and exploring the subject matter. He made the observation that individuals who establish specific, ambitious objectives surpassed those who set vague, straightforward goals. Locke drew upon Aristotle's concept of final causality as the basis for establishing goals. Locke commenced an inquiry into the impact of objectives on human conduct subsequent to Aristotle's postulation that purpose could serve as a driving force for behavior. During the 1960s, Locke dedicated his efforts to the development and enhancement of his goal-setting theory, culminating in the publication of his initial work on the subject in 1968, titled "Toward a Theory of Task Motivation and Incentives." In this seminal article, Locke effectively showcased the advantageous correlation that exists between performance and clear-cut objectives.

What precisely is your desired outcome?

There are certain items that an individual may desire, such as tickets to a theatrical performance or a combination of dinner and a cinematic experience. Conversely, there are essential necessities that are imperative, such as securing a shelter, ensuring electricity in one's residence, and having access to fuel for commuting to their place of employment. With diligent oversight of your expenses, it is possible to incorporate both into your budget whilst also setting aside funds for unforeseen circumstances.

For comprehensive insights on effectively managing financial needs and desires, please continue perusing.

Determining needs

Financial needs encompass the expenditures that are necessary for one's sustenance and professional endeavors. These are the recurring expenses such as mortgage payments, rent, or automobile insurance premiums that are inclined to encompass a significant proportion of your earnings.

Presented below is an inventory of several customary expenditures falling within the category of essential necessities:

- Residential accommodation.
- Conveyance.
- Coverage.
- Natural gas and electric energy.
- Cuisine.

Identifying one's desired objectives" or "Discovering the desired outcome

Investing in desires facilitates a more comfortable lifestyle. They are the commodities acquired for the sake of enjoyment or amusement. While it is possible to endure without them, possessing them contributes to a heightened level of gratification in life. Food is an essential requirement for sustenance, yet indulging in restaurant lunches on a daily basis is likely more of a discretionary choice.

Common desires often consist of items such as:

- Tourism.
- Amusement.
- High-end or couture clothing.
- Enrollments for fitness facilities.
- Beverages typically served in coffeehouses.

Individuals' needs and desires may vary across the board. For instance, you may have a need for an automobile to commute to your workplace on a daily basis, however, the specific type or model of car required for this purpose may undergo alterations. For example, if one's occupation entails transporting affluent clientele, the utilization of a high-end automobile may be indispensable. If your sole purpose is commuting to and from the office, a car with better fuel efficiency would suffice.

The aforementioned statement also applies to more affordable items, such as the recently released coat that has caught your attention. Whilst it is essential to possess appropriate attire to shield oneself from inclement conditions, when considering your possession of three jackets already, it becomes apparent that acquiring an additional one would be classified more as a desire rather than a necessity.

The Optimal Strategy For Establishing A Budget That Ensures Consistency

Initially, it is imperative that we commence by addressing the fundamental aspects and take cognizance of how you managed to formulate a financial plan in the initial instance.

Step by step instructions to establish out Your Spending plan.

Some individuals refrain from initiating the planning process due to concerns about its difficulty. However, it is indeed these four distinct stages.

1. Add your pay.

Expenditure commences concurrent with receipt of your payment. The entirety of it. This includes your regular checks as well as any supplementary payments received through activities such as a secondary source of income, garage sales, freelance work, and similar endeavors.

2. Rundown Your Costs.

Next, proceed to articulate your expenses. Commence with what is commonly referred to as the Four Dividers (the fundamental elements): sustenance, amenities, shelter, and conveyance. Next, proceed to incorporate additional amenities such as television streaming services, dining establishments, subscription boxes, personal expenditures, and similar offerings.

3. Financial plan to nothing.

This should not imply that you exhaust your entire financial resources and end up with empty bank accounts by the end of the month. This statement suggests that you allocate all of your financial resources towards a specific purpose, creating a designated place for each dollar earned within your budget. The strategy involved in this process is known as zero-based planning. Here is an outline of its typical functioning: Begin by listing all your expenses, subtract them from your income, and if there is any remaining surplus, allocate it towards your current financial objective. This approach allows for effective allocation of resources.

4. Track your costs.

This final progress holds paramount importance. Track. Each. Cost. When making a purchase, please ensure to record the transaction under the appropriate expense category. This is commonly the approach taken to direct one's attention towards something. Planning is the manner in which one puts forth their proposed course of action. Below is a step-by-step guide on how to proceed with the arrangement.

If you are interested in establishing budgets that you will adhere to, there are two additional resources that you should take into consideration. The fundamental aspect we previously alluded to as our primary recommendation when adhering to your budget: Maintain authenticity. When devising your budget, ensure that it is realistic and aligned with your lifestyle. The second?

Engaging in a monthly budgeting practice ahead of each month's commencement.

In order to achieve excellence, it may be advantageous to proactively consider the future. This serves as a consistently potent source of life guidance, along with an exquisite suggestion for effective planning. Perhaps you would consider opting for a monthly replacement instead. Additionally, it would be advisable to make the necessary arrangements prior to the commencement of the month.

It is a straightforward process for every dollar. You will replicate the expenditure allocation for the present month and subsequently modify it according to your preferences. As previously mentioned, you will accommodate unexpected expenses that arise (such as the birthday of your best friend or a meeting for your book club) by reallocating funds to make room for them.

Moreover, behold! Such is the method by which one adheres to a budget—a budget imbued with purpose. You are accustomed to independently impelling yourself towards achieving objectives while maintaining harmonious coexistence within society. Given that you will undertake two tasks concurrently, it is expected that you will establish rational fiscal strategies that, in addition, facilitate a transition from your current position to your desired future state.

Hacks to Reroute Emotional Spending

While fostering mindfulness remains the paramount means to restrain impulsive spending, there exist a few techniques that can be employed to heighten the obstacles for discretionary purchases.

First and foremost, it is imperative that one refrains from allowing any website, particularly Amazon, to store their credit card details. Merely compelling oneself to go through the additional process of inputting the card number may suffice in instigating self-awareness regarding one's propensity for impulsive expenditure driven by emotions.

The second tip involves discontinuing one's subscription to promotional messages. If one does not consistently receive an influx of sales notifications in their inbox, the inclination to make a purchase will be significantly diminished.

In order to effectively manage your credit or debit card usage, consider affixing a discreet reminder onto your card, such as a small adhesive note. By doing so, each time you retrieve your card, you will be presented with a timely prompt, serving as an opportunity to reflect upon your expenditure and potentially reassess your decision.

Lastly, I would suggest incorporating the utilization of the 24-hour rule. In all instances of making a purchase, irrespective of whether it amounts to $20 or $500, it is advisable to establish a practice of observing a 24-hour waiting period. Does it still hold the same level of significance? Are you, by chance, continuing to contemplate the matter at hand? Has the sale ceased to exist? It is probable that if the expenditure was deemed unnecessary or driven by emotional impulses, it is likely to have escaped your memory the following day.

4) Develop a pragmatic strategy for effectively managing your emotional and impulsive expenditures.

Despite implementing steps 1-3 diligently and achieving consistency with these approaches, there may still be instances where impulsive or emotional expenditures prevail. Kindly proceed with making provisions in your budget for that.

Despite having a difficult day, you take solace in acquiring an aesthetically pleasing blouse from Target due to the small sense of happiness it brings.

You desire to treat the children to ice cream owing to the delightful weather conditions, yet your allocated funds for Family Activities have been depleted.

Incorporate a contingency fund into your budget to account for unforeseen circumstances.

Bear in mind, attaining perfection is not the primary objective in this context. Conversely, strive to enhance your mindfulness pertaining to instances wherein undue spending driven by emotions begins to dominate, while diligently ensuring adherence to the designated budget category for unforeseen circumstances. In this manner, your expenditure will not hinder or obstruct your crucial objectives.

5) Maintain Focus on Your Principles and Objectives

This one is critical. In our previous dialogue, we have deliberated upon the notion that impulsive and emotional expenditure often stems from weariness and tension. However, two significant emotions are often in operation.

Jealousy and guilt.

Those emotions are not correlated with genuine deficits in our lives. Alternatively, they derive from our interpersonal connections, financial circumstances, and perceptions of self-value.

The actions and priorities of others divert our attention from our own endeavors.

Upon observing your neighbor's acquisition of a new automobile, you begin to regard your own vehicle with a modified perspective.

In addition to the daily triggers that we encounter, such as the prominent display of charming Joanna Gaines home decor items at Target, which inevitably invokes thoughts of societal expectations dictating the ideal appearance of our homes.

Frequently, our environment is inclined to divert our attention from our objective. Therefore, it is essential to establish an atmosphere that serves as a constant reminder of the distinct values and priorities that hold significance for both you and your family.

Incorporate your money mantra as the wallpaper for your mobile device or prominently display your goals on the refrigerator. Construct a visual representation of the aspirations and goals that you are nurturing for the life you are actively constructing.

Make every effort to concentrate on what is of utmost importance and holds significant value to you.

This entirety serves solely as a form of training. Our primary objective is to achieve progress rather than attaining perfection.

It should be borne in mind that one's emotions might appear inconvenient and overpowering in the present moment, nevertheless, if we take a step back and give them due consideration, we will probably discover that they are offering guidance regarding the needs of our physical and spiritual well-being.

Delving into the Core of the Matter

As you engage in these exercises and commence the application of these strategies, it is probable that you will uncover something unforeseen. There is no indication of a disorder or compulsive spending issue present in your situation. You are faced with a challenge that pertains to human nature. A self-care problem.

Harmonizing your expenditure with your principles does not entail perpetually grappling with excessive spending. It entails cultivating mindfulness, allotting dedicated periods for self-preservation, and crafting an aspirational vision for the future that empowers one to resist immediate gratification.

You've got this!

Personal Financial Matters
The measure of financial success lies not in one's earnings, but in the extent to which one can retain their earnings.
It is imperative to exercise control over personal finances and effectively

manage household economics. The monthly earnings are well-known, however, the crucial aspect lies in understanding the extent and manner of expenditure.

The salary often depletes quickly, with its whereabouts becoming a mystery on a regular monthly basis. Insufficient understanding of prudent financial management impedes the accumulation of savings for a majority of individuals, as all incoming funds are swiftly depleted without a clear strategy.

Building savings constitutes a fundamental aspect in the journey towards achieving financial autonomy, and thus, this chapter will center its attention on this endeavor.

Income and expenses

My financial prosperity will be achieved through the condition wherein my earnings surpass my expenditures, while satisfying my wants.

Fundamental to financial stability is the imperative that expenditure remains below income, a principle that is theoretically logical but not consistently adhered to.

In order to effectively manage and optimize our financial situation, it is crucial to possess a comprehensive understanding of both our sources of income and our expenditures. This level of clarity enables us to discern areas in which enhancements can be made.

Obtaining information about one's income is generally straightforward, given that most individuals receive a regular salary at the conclusion of each month. Conversely, gaining insight into one's expenses is a more intricate task, especially when aiming to discern them in fine-grained detail.

Regardless of whether or not you are able to achieve savings, there is certainly potential for improvement. Please obtain a sheet of paper and categorize your income and expenses into separate columns, akin to a results account commonly employed within the business realm. It is imperative that you provide a comprehensive level of detail when creating either a monthly or annual financial report. When creating a monthly income statement, it is crucial to ensure that the proportional portion of annual expenses such as insurance, property taxes, among others, is incorporated. Failure to do so will lead to an inaccurate reflection of the financial reality.

After completing the account of the results, proceed to analyze it and ascertain its conformity with reality. In the event that a discrepancy of $300 per month arises between your income and expenditures as indicated in your financial statement, it would be advisable to allocate these $300 towards monthly savings. If this is not the case, the account lacks sufficient details.

After the establishment of the results account, what subsequent steps will be taken?

Once you have familiarized yourself with your entire income and expenses, it is advisable to endeavor to augment the income category while simultaneously reducing expenses, thereby bolstering your monthly savings.

Given the inherent intricacies of income growth, efforts shall primarily be directed towards the reduction of expenses.

While it is undeniable that augmenting one's income poses challenges, let us now explore several strategies that may be applicable to your circumstances, providing you with an opportunity to capitalize on them should they align with your needs.

Monetize unused belongings in your household by engaging in the process of selling them.

In consignment shops or on online platforms such as Craig's list or eBay, you have the opportunity to sell any items that have become obsolete or irrelevant to you, enabling you to gain a noteworthy financial benefit. This could potentially enable one to achieve cost savings should they possess an excess of unused belongings that necessitate the utilization of a storage facility to maintain them.

Composition.

You can generate income by writing on the internet, be it through the creation of ebooks or the authoring of concise articles.

Create and design a website or blog.

If you possess extensive expertise in a particular field, you have the potential to establish a website through which you can generate supplementary income.

Offer additional room rentals.

If you possess a spare room within your domicile and harbor no objections to occasional lodging of individuals therein, you have the opportunity to generate supplementary income of commendable value by engaging with platforms such as Airbnb for rental purposes.

Generate income through online initiatives such as participating in surveys, creating content for YouTube, and similar activities.

There are numerous opportunities available online to generate income, which can effectively supplement your primary employment.

Herein lies a small selection of potential means to generate additional income, with creative thinking serving as the sole constraint.

In the majority of instances, however, it will prove more feasible to minimize costs rather than to augment revenue. Frequently, individuals allocate funds towards unnecessary items and those which they scarcely desire. Hence, it becomes highly plausible to promptly eradicate such expenditures. Subsequently, we are going to witness compelling instances of the significant long-term savings that can be achieved in seemingly mundane aspects such as coffee.

Managing expenditures using an Excel spreadsheet.

Exercise caution when managing minor expenses; even the smallest leak can cause a significant impact in one's financial situation.

Funds are rapidly dissipating from your possession, and often it is the minor expenditures that bear responsibility for this. The income statement is expected to show a positive variance between revenues and expenses, while the ultimate outcome at the end of the month will result in zero savings. This can be attributed to the usual practice of excluding minor expenses when calculating overall expenditure, despite their potential to have a significant impact as illustrated by Benjamin Franklin's analogy of a sinking boat.

If one lacks precise knowledge of the exact spending amounts and their allocation, it becomes challenging to effectively enhance savings. Therefore, the most viable approach to acquire this information is by diligently monitoring and documenting all expenditures within an Excel spreadsheet, preferably over a period lasting between two to three months. The task of meticulously recording all daily expenditures for an entire month may appear laborious, yet it affords us a comprehensive understanding of the allocation of expenses. This comprehension, in turn, facilitates the identification and subsequent elimination of the customary frivolous ones experienced by all.

After identifying all the expenditures, you can categorize them to obtain a broader understanding and arrange them according to their level of importance. The most optimal approach to saving is by eliminating superfluous expenditures, specifically those that yield minimal contributions and are not inherently missed when removed from our financial habits.

One effective approach for practical implementation entails examining actual instances of expenditure among diverse individuals, enabling an identification of potential areas and corresponding quantities where cost reduction may be achieved.

The cited examples originate from individuals within my acquaintance whose expenses I oversee, and I have endeavored to accurately represent their respective data to the best of my ability. Consequently, the structure of each example might vary slightly. There exists a plethora of diverse methods to manage expenditures effectively, all of which possess equal efficacy. It is crucial to arrange it in a manner that facilitates enhanced comprehension.

Example 1. Expenses incurred by an individual failing to fulfill their rent obligations. The expenditures are classified into categories A, B, and C, with A denoting utmost importance and C representing minimal significance.

$	Costs C	$
104	Takeaway	63
40	Eating out	36
33	Pubs	70
177	**Total**	169

The aforementioned table indicates that the individual's expenses are relatively modest, totaling $759. However, there are still opportunities for further economization should it be deemed necessary. Categorized under classification C, the expenses amount to

$169 per month, a considerable sum that could potentially determine whether one saves a portion or no portion at all.

Though it is commonly enjoyable to indulge in social activities such as visiting a bar or dining out, financial constraints often inhibit our ability to partake regularly. We need not eradicate such indulgences; however, it is imperative that we exercise moderation in our expenditures to ensure some savings at the conclusion of each month. Rather than allocating $70 per month towards bar expenses and $99 towards dining out and takeout, it would be advisable for this individual to aim for half of that amount in each category. This modest adjustment should be easily attainable by exercising self-control, resulting in an extra monthly savings of $85.

$85 per month may not appear to be a substantial amount, however, cumulatively it amounts to a total of $1020 annually. For an individual with a monthly income of $1000, setting aside a seemingly modest amount of $85 per month translates to accumulating an entire month's salary within a year, a factor that warrants consideration. Our main character could, for instance, request an unpaid leave of absence for one month annually to unwind, by decreasing their frequenting of bars and restaurants.

At what point ought this individual contemplate the reduction of expenditures?

If the protagonist is earning, for instance, a monthly income of $2000, there is no imperative to curtail expenses, since relinquishing all indulgences would result in saving a mere additional $169- a sum that does not carry substantial ramifications if one is already setting aside $1000 monthly. On the contrary, if your monthly income amounts to $800, your savings would effectively be negligible given these expenditures. It is highly recommended to explore the possibility of reducing expenses in order to commence building a financial buffer against unforeseen circumstances.

Example 2. Costs incurred by a childless young couple who are responsible for rent payments. The expenditures during two distinct months, one characterized by substantial expenses and minimal savings for the couple, and another marked by increased savings.

I encountered a month devoid of any savings.

Expenditures $ Revenue Savings

The amount has been resolved to 747.74, with a total of 2,270 occurrences and a rate of 3.35.

The cost of food amounts to $260.79.

Requires 577

The aforementioned amount consists of desires totaling 669.62.

Surprising outcome of 11.5 percent was observed.

The cumulative sum amounts to 2266.65.

Month with savings

Expenditures $ Revenue Savings

830.6 has been adjusted to 809.02, with an initial value of 2270.

The cost of food amounts to $117.17.

Requires a total of 285.87 units.

Demands a sum of 227.34
Surprising
The overall sum amounts to 1460.98.

Fixed obligations comprise of monthly expenses such as rental payment, internet and telephone charges, utility bills, and gym membership fees. The requirements encompass elements such as transportation, fuel, apparel, and sustenance, while the preferences encompass superfluous attire, cuisine, or journeys, among other things.

The earnings of this couple are not exorbitant; however, their meticulous cost control measures, demonstrated by detailed data in each category, prove to be a significantly more significant contributing factor.

There exist couples whose total earnings amount to $5,000, however, they are unable to accumulate any savings by the end of the month. In contrast, our main characters are able to save over $800 during months with minimal expenses, which equates to a noteworthy 35% of their income. As this couple's income gradually increases to $5,000, they will persist in adhering to the same ideology and will likely find it effortless to save 35% of their income, equivalent to approximately $1750 per month. Such a significant level of savings will rapidly propel them towards achieving financial independence.

Fixed costs, necessities, and sustenance represent expenditures that are arduous to circumvent. Despite the potential for discovering more economical means of dining or engaging in physical activity, it remains vital to reside comfortably and derive pleasure from one's daily existence. The desires are the primary determinant that distinguishes the act of saving from not saving, and as such, they are the foremost aspect to be regulated.

The couple possesses the means to undertake activities such as travel and dining out without facing financial difficulties. However, it is beyond their reach to indulge in these pursuits on a monthly basis, as they consistently adhere to a budget that does not exceed their earnings. If this couple were to continue their monthly spending patterns as depicted in the initial table, they would find themselves toiling for numerous years, only to eventually deplete their savings entirely. Such a financial course would render them highly susceptible to any unexpected economic circumstances and inevitably necessitate a lifetime of labor.

In essence, the aforementioned couple exhibits a highly favorable financial situation, as they are able to save 35% of their earnings during months of prosperity. Although they have experienced challenges in saving during certain months, they possess the capability to maintain a harmonious equilibrium between indulging in leisure and impulsive desires while also saving. Furthermore, it is possible that as their income grows, so too will their capacity to save, as it is presumed that their expenditure will not increase proportionately. If they were to deploy those savings by making investments, as we will discuss in more detail later, each passing day would bring them nearer to achieving financial security, alleviating concerns about money.

It is a matter of prioritization." "Prioritization is key." "Everything revolves around setting priorities." "Priorities are paramount.

While certain individuals perceive frequent dining out as fundamental, others may view it as frivolous, preferring to prioritize expenditure on membership at a premium fitness facility. All positions command equal respect; however, it is simply not feasible to prioritize everything. If we prioritize the consideration of all costs, it will render saving and breaking free from the cycle of endless work unattainable. Hence, it behooves us all to be prepared to potentially reduce expenditure within category C.

In the event of job loss, it is conceivable that adjustments to one's expenditure may be made in order to live within the confines of a $1000 monthly budget. Thus, it becomes plausible to achieve this accommodating lifestyle without necessitating job loss. Begin with modest steps, by ceasing all expenditures that afford you minimal pleasure, and observe how, at the conclusion of the month, you will have accumulated additional funds, without feeling any sense of deprivation from refraining from these purchases or activities.

A number of years ago, I frequently availed myself of food-to-go on multiple occasions within a week, resulting in a significant monthly expenditure. Presently, I exercise self-discipline, limiting my indulgence to a maximum of once per week, thereby ensuring substantial savings and meeting my financial obligations. This concept, when applied across various expenditures, may determine whether one ends up with a negative cash flow or manages to accumulate significant savings.

The objective is not to eradicate all minor indulgences and adopt a destitute lifestyle, but rather to exercise restraint in spending and avoid emulating affluent individuals without possessing similar means.

Commissions

In relation to commissions, it is recommended to carefully assess the values associated with the investments you intend to utilize frequently. You will be required to pay brokerage fees for your investment transactions; it is crucial to carefully monitor the commissions associated with your chosen investments.

Certain brokerages may impose charges for the acquisition of mutual funds, but it is possible to select a brokerage that facilitates mutual fund transactions without any associated fees. (Please note that the application of expense ratios is determined by the fund itself, not the broker. Exchange-Traded Funds (ETFs) are subject to brokerage commissions due to their share prices, which function similarly to those of stocks.)

Nonetheless, in the event that you opt for mutual funds devoid of transaction fees or ETFs without any commissions, it is possible to acquire mutual fund bonds and ETFs without incurring any expenses. However, it is worth noting that individual bonds may have charges, in accordance with the predetermined minimum and maximum amounts, established by your brokerage. When endeavoring to locate a suitable broker, one can achieve cost savings by bypassing the imposition of commission fees. Seek out a broker who provides a fee-free alternative.

Promotions / Incentives

Brokers endeavor to provide customers with encouragement to engage in business with them, thereby frequently organizing promotional events. While the primary factor in selecting a broker should not be solely based on a favorable promotion, it can possibly serve as a decisive factor in cases where making a final decision proves challenging. Certain entities may provide a monetary incentive upon the deposit of a predetermined sum, whereas others may elect to exempt commission fees for a designated quantity of transactions. Brokerages that have affiliations with financial institutions may also extend a reduced rate to clients who maintain an active checking account. Regardless of the circumstances, it is essential to take into account both the immediate and extended consequences. Ultimately, the offer loses its appeal when one becomes burdened by exorbitant trade commissions subsequent to the expiration of the promotional period.

Optimizing the Selection of an Appropriate Account.

The process of choosing an appropriate brokerage account does not have to be a cumbersome endeavor. Initially, it is imperative to ascertain the type of account that aligns with your preferences. Afterwards, you may proceed to evaluate and contrast different brokers to determine the one that best suits your specific requirements. The choice of a brokerage account can be contingent upon your specific investment objectives. In order to ascertain the most optimal course of action, one must contemplate their objectives.

If your objective is to allocate funds for purposes of building a financial cushion, or if you have a near-term objective, it is highly probable that a conventional brokerage account would be necessary. While it may be necessary for you to fulfill tax obligations in relation to the dividends and profits earned from your investment, it is important to note that you retain the flexibility to withdraw your funds at any moment. Additionally, it is possible to establish a cash account where you will be given the option to avail margin privileges. This will allow you to obtain loans for purchasing stocks, with the stocks in your existing portfolio serving as collateral. However, there are potential hazards involved, necessitating the payment of interest on any borrowed funds.

On the flip side, your objectives could be oriented towards the long term. If your primary goal is to accumulate funds for your retirement, an Individual Retirement Account (IRA) presents itself as the most apparent and advantageous option. By utilizing a Traditional IRA, individuals are eligible to receive tax deductions when making contributions but are required to defer accessing their funds until reaching 59.5 years of age. A Roth IRA does not offer a tax deduction upon contribution, but it allows for tax-exempt withdrawals. Furthermore, it is feasible to make withdrawals from your Roth contributions, excluding the earnings, at any given point. For individuals who work for themselves, opting for a SEP-IRA, SIMPLE IRA, or individual 401(k) would be the most suitable course of action.

Opening an Account

After the careful selection of a broker and the suitable account that aligns with your requirements, it is now time to proceed to the subsequent stage. You are prepared to commence the establishment of a brokerage account.

Initially, you will be required to complete an application for the establishment of a new account, a task which can be conveniently executed through online means. It will be necessary to provide information in order to authenticate your identity, therefore, kindly keep your social security and driver's license numbers readily accessible. You will furnish financial information primarily pertaining to your net worth, investment objectives, assets, and employment particulars.

Following that, you will transfer funds into your newly established account. Typically, there exist several alternatives to achieve this objective; the choice of which is contingent upon your broker. A wire transfer is considered the most expeditious method (taking only a few minutes) to deposit funds into your account, as the monetary value is instantaneously transferred from one banking institution to another. Additionally, it is possible to establish an electronic funds transfer (EFT) mechanism that enables the seamless movement of funds from either a savings or checking account. This task typically requires one working day to finish. It is also feasible to execute a transfer of existing investments held with an alternate broker or to rollover a 401(k) account, commonly referred to as an asset transfer. Furthermore, it is typically possible to issue a check, although it may require a few days for the funds to become accessible.

It is important to keep in mind that there may exist different minimum requirements, depending on the specific type of account. Please ensure that you are attentive to the minimum requirements set by your broker.

Now that you have successfully established your new account, you can commence the process of conducting investment research. The cumulative efforts you have invested until this point have brought you to this juncture, compelling you to initiate the construction of a multifaceted financial portfolio. Allocate a portion of your time to acquainting yourself with the methods of responsibly selecting stocks, bonds, and funds.

The Pervasive Benefits Of Possessing An Inquisitive Nature

In the world of business, curiosity is frequently perceived as a catalyst for change, as it prompts individuals to scrutinize established processes and evaluate their efficacy in attaining organizational goals. Entrepreneurs often exhibit reluctance to critically examine their operational methods, subscribing to the adage that suggests one need not address issues unless they are overtly malfunctioning. Nonetheless, deferring the evaluation of one's strategies and procedures until a crisis manifests can prove calamitous.

The formal way to express the same idea is: Curiosity can be defined as possessing an innate inquisitiveness and an intrinsic motivation to acquire knowledge or understanding. A curious entrepreneur demonstrates a propensity for comprehending the underlying reasons and motivations for their decisions prior to delving into the specific actions. For instance, upon reaching the six-month mark in your business, you might determine the desire to secure a lease for an office space to serve as your operational base. However, a curious mindset would compel you to first investigate the rationale behind this inclination to lease an office space. Is it primarily due to the expansion of your operations, rendering your garage inadequate for running your business, or is it the prevailing expectation among accomplished entrepreneurs to operate from a designated office space that is compelling you to make this choice? Upon conducting a thorough analysis and delving into your decision, you have the opportunity to gain insights into your underlying motivations, potentially resulting in significant financial savings.

Moreover, curiosity holds further advantages as it facilitates the opportunity to question and confront one's own ideas. Now, you may be pondering the reasons behind why it would be advantageous for you to question your ideas. Consider approaching this matter from a different perspective: Prior to the advent of smartphones, individuals needed to acquire digital cameras in order to capture exquisite photographs, make handwritten notes of their tasks, and procure printed editions of books. This singular innovation enabled us to integrate numerous facets of our lives into a single device. By refraining from questioning the established norms and exploring unconventional perspectives, enterprises would not be able to drive innovation in sectors and revolutionize the typical lifestyle.

Steve Jobs exemplifies a leadership style characterized by persistent questioning and scrutiny of his ideas, leading to the development of groundbreaking products that revolutionized the way individuals communicate and engage with technology. In 2007, following the successful launch of the Macintosh computer and the iPod, Steve Jobs unveiled his newest creation that amalgamated three groundbreaking products into a single device:

Today, we are pleased to unveil three unprecedented products within this category. The initial device is a widescreen iPod with touch controls, whereas the second one is an innovative cellular phone, and the third one represents a significant advancement in internet communications. Therefore, there are three entities to be discussed, namely a wide display iPod featuring touch-based controls, an innovative cellular device, and a pioneering internet communication apparatus. These entities are not disparate apparatus. This is one device. We are formally designating this product as the iPhone. (Guglielmo, 2017)

The iPhone not only rectified a communication dilemma, but it also facilitated the recognition of previously unknown consumer requirements. Prior to this realization, it was not widely understood that the demand of consumers was for the convenience of instant internet access at their fingertips, as opposed to the traditional process of booting up a computer. Indeed, it can be inferred that Steve Jobs and his team possessed a keen curiosity, allowing them to envision the forthcoming technological realm and its profound impact on the realm of communication.

Inquisitiveness serves as a potent asset as it empowers you to pose inquiries that engender novel solutions, consequently enhancing the efficacy of your organizational procedures. Rather than accepting the status quo or adhering to industry norms, you have the opportunity to innovate your products and services by synthesizing disparate concepts or adopting methodologies from unrelated sectors. Maintaining a sense of curiosity can further facilitate the process of thoughtfully and deliberately making decisions. Prior to finalizing a task, it is advisable to evaluate if its investment of time and financial resources is justified or if it contributes towards accomplishing your immediate objectives.

Below are several inquiries focused on enhancing business operations that you may consider posing to yourself or your team in order to surpass current limitations and nurture innovative thinking:

What is the primary factor impeding the generation of heightened revenue? What strategies can be implemented to enhance existing operational processes and drive increased profitability within the company?

What are some of the potential avenues that you can explore in the current market landscape? Are there any strategic measures that you can adopt in order to enhance the market share of your business?

What is the single requirement that our esteemed clientele lacks awareness about? In what manner can you enhance your offerings or services in order to effectively cater to this underlying, subconscious requirement?

What strategies can be employed to acquire a larger customer base without escalating the marketing expenditure? What alternative strategies can be implemented to increase product sales without introducing new products?

What internal processes require reevaluation and restructuring? How can the implementation of technology enhance your operational agility?

Chapter 1

Are you prepared to take charge of your financial affairs?

The title of this book may cause perplexity since, undoubtedly, the fact that you are perusing its contents indicates your preparedness. Nevertheless, while that may be technically true, many individuals are willing to explore prospects that are uncertain in terms of their commitment and financial management. If one is not adequately prepared to handle their finances, they will be unable to take the requisite steps towards doing so. To commence, it is advisable to acquire an understanding of one's financial status and consider indicators that signify the necessity of implementing fiscal management strategies. There are unquestionably evident indicators that necessitate the management of your finances, acquisition of a novel money management system, or perhaps the acquisition of new knowledge to enhance your abilities in this domain. In the following chapter, we will delve into a selection of these instances, aiming not only to identify them but also to provide insight into potential areas for improvement that can be rectified at a later stage.

1. One lacks knowledge regarding the destination of their money. 2. Your understanding of the allocation of your finances is limited. 3. The whereabouts of one's money remains unknown to them.

Prior to acquiring any proficiency in financial planning, I was oblivious to my expenditure patterns. Nevertheless, upon assuming management of it, I discerned the underlying issue. I was indulging in excessive spending without any established financial goals, thus making impulsive purchases primarily driven by emotional impulses.

Since assuming the role of manager, I have cultivated a heightened sense of attentiveness and have even taken the initiative of engaging a professional to handle my receipt organization. Consequently, this affords me a comprehensive overview of my expenditures, including precise details pertaining to timing and the nature of each transaction. If you encounter a similar issue, it is imperative to initiate measures to effectively supervise it in order to gain a comprehensive understanding of its trajectory and establish mechanisms for regulation.

2. Insufficient funds at the conclusion of the month.

If one becomes aware that their funds are depleted before fulfilling all crucial obligations, it is imperative for them to embark upon enhancing their aptitude for financial administration. This situation could indicate a significant amount of impulsive spending or, alternatively, it might indicate a need for lifestyle simplification. Both of these tasks can be accomplished through the application of appropriate financial expertise.

3. It is devoid of enjoyment

Consider the following perspective: If you were to acquire a brand new automobile and an individual inquired about it, your response would likely be one of enthusiasm, accompanied by a cheerful expression. However, how do you react when the topic of finances arises? Does it elicit enthusiasm, cultivate a sense of joy, or evoke a desire for diversion, or alternatively, instill a feeling of trepidation. If such is indeed the circumstance, there appears to be an aspect of your finances that you find unsatisfactory.

I previously held aversion towards the subject matter, but upon self-reflection, I determined that my frustration did not stem from the monetary aspect per se, but rather from the manner in which I was handling it. The financial statements were disorganized, lacking clear direction and occasionally experiencing improper distribution. Nevertheless, after achieving a level of proficiency in managing it, I developed a genuine enthusiasm for discussing and overseeing it.

4. Your primary purpose for existence is to meet your financial obligations.

Every day, you diligently engage in the routine of going to work, nourishing your body, enjoying restful slumber, and fulfilling financial obligations. It appears that allocating your financial resources in such a manner has become a prevailing tendency lately. However, what I discovered a few years ago is that the issue lies not in your insufficient earnings, but rather in the inadequacy of your system to account for other expenses or goals. Indeed, although the bills may appear significant, once control over one's finances is effectively achieved, expenditures inexplicably diminish, leading to a gradual reduction in expenses.

5. Your financial situation is a cause of anxiety.

If you consistently struggle with meeting payment deadlines, perpetually being concerned about potential card rejection, prolonging outstanding balances on your credit cards, incurring frequent overdraft fees, and possessing a meager sum of less than $100, it is evident that something is amiss. It is imperative to proactively adopt a fresh perspective and initiate a transformation in your behavior and routines. As eloquently stated by a distinguished intellectual, it is an undeniable truth that an individual cannot successfully resolve a predicament using the very same mindset that brought it forth. These challenges can solely be resolved by acquiring novel knowledge, expertise, and discernment. In actuality, money has the potential to provide immense satisfaction rather than causing distress.

Having perused the preceding page, if you believe you have acquired sufficient information and are prepared to embark on the journey towards enhancing your fiscal discipline, we shall proceed forthwith.

Chapter 3: Keeping Track

If the $1000.00, which has been marked as "changing out" or removed from your record, is subsequently spent on various purchases, while the landowner deposits the check in their bank together with your March lease, you will encounter the issue of bounced checks.

Checks are believed to be beneficial for a duration of up to six months. To ensure that a check cannot be cashed by another party, it is advisable to pursue one of the following options: a) retrieve the physical check and render it void, or b) remit a payment of $20.00 (or more) to the bank, utilizing the "Stop Check" service, thereby preventing the recipient from accessing the assumed value of the check. Occasionally, financial institutions may honor checks that surpass the 6-month timeframe, while regrettably, there are limited recourses available to address the situation if the check in question was not forged. This is yet another remarkable incentive to ensure you are well-informed of the bank's knowledge and that you diligently oversee the organization of your records.

They are currently meandering in an uncertain location, and have not been redeemed thus far.

You may also choose to contact the property manager and request that they promptly deposit the check, alleviating any further concerns on your part. Calling can

Occasionally, we would like to inform you that the check has been misplaced.

in

The correspondence may have been misplaced or overlooked within someone's office storage. If the loss of your check was indeed caused by your landlord, it is only fair that they bear the financial responsibility of $20.00 for the stop payment expense so that you may issue a replacement check without incurring double payment.

WARNING: Please be advised that despite the payment of a stop check fee, the stoppage will only remain effective for a period of six months. In exceptional cases, there may arise situations where a check shall be reimbursed from your bank account beyond the six-month period. However, it is expected that the bank shall diligently ensure the return of your funds, in the event such circumstances materialize.

IMPORTANT: On certain occasions, in the event that you maintain minimal funds within your account and the bank erroneously deducts an amount that you believe to be a mistake, you may encounter the unfortunate situation of issuing insufficient funds checks and incurring associated fees. However, if it is understood by the bank that they have made an error, a bank representative should be prepared to: a) waive any outstanding charges that you may owe, and b) communicate with the relevant parties, such as the grocery store, to reimburse them for any expenses that you may be liable for due to the bounced check. Please ensure to make a formal request to the bank for payment of the store charges in the event that the bank is found responsible.

Using Credit Cards

Credit can be viewed as an alternative term for 'loan.' Every dollar obtained through layaway carries an accompanying responsibility to repay, including the cost of utilizing borrowed funds (often referred to as 'interest.') Mastercard presents an enticing proposition wherein credit transactions are rendered effortless. Merely procure desired items and allocate the charges to the card, subsequently fulfilling a modest monthly obligation of $10.00 or $15.00. This remarkable arrangement serves as an exceptional means of dispensing finances.

The Profit Generation Methods of Credit Card Companies

Credit card institutions do not operate with the intention of providing individuals with complimentary funds; rather, their purpose lies in generating revenue. They employ two primary methodologies to accomplish this: firstly, by imposing a fee on the establishment for utilizing their service, typically amounting to 2% or a higher percentage of the total purchase price; and secondly, by imposing an interest penalty upon you in the event that you fail to promptly repay the amount owed to them. Typically, a substantial amount of interest is charged annually, ranging from 15% to 24.99% or potentially higher.

Therefore, in the event that you make the decision to acquire that shirt or pair of pants at the price of $45.00 and opt to use your Visa credit card for the transaction, the store will be required to remit approximately $1.00 to the Mastercard organization as a fee, in order to facilitate your use of the Visa credit card. Subsequently, if you do not repay the Visa organization the entire sum of $45.00 within the designated month, you will be liable to pay interest to the Visa organization.

Understanding the Mechanism of Credit Card Interest Rates

Therefore, you have acquired the trousers for a discounted price of $45.00, which was subsequently reflected in the invoice issued by the Mastercard consortium. As per the terms, you fulfilled the payment obligation by remitting their standard fee of $10.00. You are actually indebted to the Visa company.

pany $35.00. During the initial month, you will incur a certain amount of interest.

— suppose $.70.

In the upcoming month, you will acquire an additional pair of pants based on the premise that they are

Given the circumstances, it appears that you are interested in acquiring an additional pair which, regrettably, is not available at a discounted price. Thus, the cost of the second pair would amount to $65.00. You made the purchase using your credit

card. The total amount payable for your credit card bill is $100.70, comprising the principal sum of $35.00, an additional interest charge of $0.70, and a separate charge of $65.00. You are required to remit the foundational amount.

The amount due is $12.00, with a remaining balance of $88.70.

The charge card organization will promptly enhance your advantage. They will not solely impose revenue on the actual amount charged by you ($35.00 $65.00 - $12.00 = $88.00). Interest will be applied to your previous purchases, your future purchases, and the interest that has already been accrued. An interest fee will be applied to the amount of $100.70. The interest accrued during that period would amount to $1.75, resulting in a total balance of $90.45. Currently, the pants that had a price reduction of $45.00 are effectively priced $2.45 higher.

In the upcoming month, you shall acquire footwear and outerwear, which you shall put on your Mastercard account, amounting to a maximum of $220.00. Subsequently, upon receiving your bill from the Mastercard institution, you will remit a payment of $15.00. You have not fully settled the outstanding balance for the initial pair of pants, and additionally, you have not made any payments towards the subsequent pair of pants, as well as the shoes and coat. As a result, the total amount owed now stands at $90.45 for the first pair of pants and $220.00 for the remaining items, resulting in a combined outstanding balance of $310.45. The aforementioned monthly benefit amounts to $5.90, thereby keeping your credit card charge at a total of $316.35. By making a payment of exactly $15.00, you will be able to reduce your outstanding Mastercard balance to $301.35.

Furthermore, after the course of three months, you have yet to finalize the payment process for the initial pair of pants acquired at a discounted price. Unexpectedly and without prior notice, a balance of zero dollars and zero cents appeared.

Given the 90-day time frame, your total outstanding balance of $301.35 has accumulated, and attempting to make a

lump sum payment within a single month is not feasible.
your money flow!
Well, that is a matter that should not be trifled with, one might surmise. If you were to persistently continue making additional purchases without making regular and fair minimum payments, you would gradually accumulate a larger debt to the credit card company and incur increasingly significant amounts of accrued interest. Therefore so
Multiple undergraduate students, upon receiving their initial visas at the age of 18, often incur significant credit card debt amounting to thousands of dollars before they reach the age of 19. Mastercard organizations love that. They earn substantial amounts of money.

Chapter Thirteen: Capital Allocation in Real Estate
The most significant financial undertaking one typically engages in throughout one's lifetime is the acquisition of a personal residence.
Introduction

Real estate, much like equity investments, serves as a growth-oriented asset with the potential to significantly contribute to the creation of wealth in the long run. Additionally, it enables the utilization of bank financing to acquire real estate assets, such as physical properties, that appreciate in value over time and generate rental revenue.

What are the reasons to consider making an investment in real estate?

Real estate serves as a long-term investment vehicle, leading to appreciation in value over an extended period. You might consider making a financial investment in your own residence or purchasing a property for the purpose of investment. Additionally, it is worth noting that in order to acquire a loan from a banking institution to procure the property, a mere 10% deposit is obligatory. Subsequently, you can procure a lessee who will assume responsibility for a majority or the entirety of the monthly bond payments, while you may be required to bear the costs of rates and levies. In due course, you will possess a appreciating asset in which you have only made partial contributions, notwithstanding the necessity of attending to additional preliminary expenses.

What are the various categories of real estate?

Property asset classes commonly encompass various types of properties such as offices, shopping centers, industrial real estate, warehouses, retirement communities, medical facilities, hotels, and similar establishments. Listed property funds, which are publicly listed on the stock exchange, provide individuals with a vehicle to obtain exposure to these properties.

What are the various methods for investing in real estate?

An individual has the opportunity to make investments in real estate. For instance, the aforementioned encompasses tangible assets and shares affiliated with listed properties, specifically property corporations listed on the Johannesburg Stock Exchange (JSE). A property fund pertains to a mutual fund that allocates its investments towards publicly traded companies that specialize in real estate. It affords individuals the chance to diversify their property investments by acquiring a solitary stock.

What are the benefits associated with investing in listed property?
Purchasing shares in publicly listed real estate grants individuals, regardless of their limited investment capacity, the chance to acquire property ownership. Investing in publicly listed real estate enables individuals to embark on a process of accumulating savings and generating moderate returns. Liquidity is an essential element when it comes to investing in publicly traded real estate assets. Shares in real estate assets offer higher levels of liquidity compared to fixed property investments, thus facilitating swift and effortless

transactions during selling and purchasing processes. Investing in publicly traded real estate shares entails lower risk as it involves a diversified portfolio of multiple properties rather than singular property investment. There is no need for concern regarding property maintenance and tenant acquisition, as these tasks are assumed by the competent management teams of the registered property enterprises. Additionally, it is common for the majority of listed property companies to distribute regular dividends to their shareholders on a biannual basis.

What are the merits of allocating funds towards tangible assets?

In terms of short-term stability, physical assets exhibit lower volatility compared to listed assets, as there is a daily fluctuation in the value of shares on the stock market. Real estate possessions possess an inherent sentimental value due to their tangible nature; the sight of one's property brings about a sense of contentment and satisfaction. Residential real estate is highly sought after by individuals seeking entry into the market. If you possess a primary, enduring debt with financial institutions, it affords you the opportunity to establish a credit history, facilitating your eligibility for a supplemental financial instrument, thereby granting you entry into the investment property market.

What steps should be taken to initiate property investment?

Real estate holds value as a wise and enduring financial commitment. One can initiate their investment journey by opting for either the acquisition of listed property shares or SA REITs (real estate investment trusts), or by purchasing a singular property asset such as an apartment or building and gradually expanding from there. There exist multiple approaches to accomplish this task; however, it does necessitate a considerable amount of time. The concept of fractional property ownership, whether it involves the ownership of a single hotel room or shares in publicly listed properties, has demonstrated notable success and resilience. The property has exhibited long-term stability, and it is anticipated that it will continue to experience favorable progress in the future.

What are the determinants of property affordability?

The cost of a property and the prevailing interest rate on your mortgage loan are significant factors to take into account. Can you still manage the cost of your home when there is an increase in the interest rates? As an investor, are you financially capable of making your bond payments in the event that your property remains unoccupied, and if so, for what duration? What is your creditworthiness?

What is the optimal approach for acquiring real estate?

Possible alternative in a formal tone: "Alternative possibilities encompass collaborative partnerships, joint ventures, structured financial arrangements, as well as seeking support and involvement from familial, Stokvel, or angelic (external) benefactors." Purchasing property off-plan is a viable option as it allows for securing the price at the onset of the development. Furthermore, there is no obligation to pay transfer duty in the event of purchasing a property off-plan. Distressed properties may also be acquired from financial institutions aiming to reclaim properties from clients in default or from properties in estates of deceased individuals.

What steps can be taken to ensure success in property investment?

There exist numerous variables that could exert influence on the success of individual investments. Both buyers and current landlords have the option to enlist the assistance of professional agents in the selection and oversight of rental properties. Furthermore, it is recommended that rental management agents be engaged to conduct the necessary ongoing and exit inspections of rental properties as mandated by the

Rental Housing Act. These items entail an expense.

What are the key considerations that contribute to the attractiveness of property investment?

The decreased interest rates enable individuals to secure a housing loan with greater ease and successfully manage the monthly installments.
Decreased property values due to a surge in property listings by owners and investors who are unable to sustain ownership and intend to promptly sell them.
There is an increase in the demand for rental properties from individuals who are currently unable to afford a purchase or simply have a preference for not doing so.

What are the Benefits of Property Investment?

It represents a favorable means to initiate the accumulation of individual financial assets. In addition to ensuring long-term occupancy, a residence possesses great utility as an asset, which, as you progressively repay it, can serve as collateral for securing your children's education, mitigating medical crises, or embarking on additional real estate ventures.

What is the optimal property size to consider for investment purposes?

Typically, one-bedroom and studio apartments exhibit favorable potential as investments in the buy-to-let market. Acquiring aged properties and undertaking extensive renovations with the objective of enhancing their value is an alternative approach.
Sectional title properties in South Africa enjoy strong performance due to their high demand among prospective homeowners entering the market for the first time. Gated communities exhibit favorable performance due to heightened emphasis on security. Diversifying your property investments

across various locations is an effective strategy to safeguard your portfolio against the impacts of market volatility.

What level of financial resources is necessary to acquire the property?

To commence, it is necessary to provide an initial payment, commonly referred to as a deposit, which typically amounts to approximately 10% of the total property price. Furthermore, it will be necessary to secure financial resources, typically in the form of a mortgage provided by a banking institution. It is advantageous to explore different options when seeking the most favorable interest rate. Additionally, there is a myriad of other expenses for which one must allocate funds, including transfer duties (if applicable), conveyancing costs, levies, and so forth. These concepts will be further deliberated upon within subsequent sections of this chapter.

Fundamental Principles of Budgeting: A Comprehensive Overview and Significance

In essence, budgeting entails the systematic development of a comprehensive breakdown outlining the inflow and outflow of financial resources over a designated timeframe. Envision a budget as a balance, with one side representing your earnings and the other side comprising a detailed breakdown of your expenditure patterns. To ensure your financial serenity, it is imperative that the expenses do not exceed or surpass the income side in the detailed breakdown of your financial transactions. A budget is instrumental in facilitating the determination of whether one should dine at their preferred restaurant or return home to prepare a meal. The conventional approach to budgeting involved utilizing either a spreadsheet or the manual method of pen and paper. Nonetheless, in contemporary times, numerous online resources and mobile/computer applications have emerged, which facilitate the budgeting process with remarkable convenience. The rationale for implementing a budget lies in the creation of a comprehensive, structured, and tangible strategy to effectively allocate funds and facilitate the tracking of financial inflows and outflows. Budgeting enables individuals to allocate and utilize their financial resources in a manner that prioritizes areas crucial to achieving financial tranquility.

In essence, budgeting entails the process of aligning your earnings and expenditures to gain clarity on the appropriate allocation of your financial resources. For instance, in the absence of a comprehensive budget that facilitates a thorough comprehension of your financial situation, it is conceivable to succumb to impulsive purchases, thereby potentially undermining the integrity of your monthly expenditure plan. It constitutes a preliminary framework for the subsequent expenditure. There exists a distinction between creating a financial plan and maintaining a record of expenses. The latter facilitates the monitoring of daily expenditure, whereas the former is intended for premeditating financial allocation prior to its actual utilization.

Exercise caution to avoid erroneously conflating factual information.

Statement: The reality is that budgeting alone does not result in the complete eradication of one's financial difficulties. Budgeting is a roadmap. It serves as a means of monitoring one's financial expenditures, constituting a pivotal stride towards establishing financial soundness and stability. One advantage lies in the fact that regardless of whether you decide to employ the notebook approach or take advantage of the various budgeting applications and software available online, the process of budgeting remains straightforward. For the majority of individuals, formulating a budget is a straightforward task, whereas adhering to it proves to be significantly challenging.

Engaging in the practice of budgeting and diligently overseeing your financial resources will enable you to discern areas within your lifestyle that involve frivolous spending. Consequently, you will acquire the ability to evade such tendencies and efficiently align your income with your desired financial objectives. Upon initially documenting your budget, you will be astonished by the various avenues through which your finances dissipate. It may come as a surprise to you that your expenditure on entertainment actually surpasses that on food. Conversely, you will acquire insight into the disparity between your expenditures on junk food versus those on nutritious options. The incapacity to accurately ascertain your expenses is a significant contributing factor to the financial difficulties and challenges you are facing. Developing a budget can be instrumental in mitigating financial anxiety by providing a structured approach to your finances, thereby alleviating stress and promoting a sense of preparedness. By implementing a comprehensive financial strategy, one can eliminate any uncertainty regarding the availability of funds for essential expenses such as food, transportation, and other vital outlays. This ensures that financial planning guarantees the presence of adequate funds before any expenditure takes place.

A budget centers on three fundamental principles: your earnings, expenses, and financial objectives. Supremely significant, a budget must possess the quality of being grounded in reality above all else. What constitutes an unfeasible or implausible budget? Allow us to examine an illustrative instance. A budget that does not accurately capture all your expenses can be deemed as unrealistic. As an illustration, allotting $100 for food expenses despite consistently surpassing that amount would render your budget impractical and exceedingly difficult to adhere to. Maintaining a frugal lifestyle resembles shedding excess weight - challenging yet immensely rewarding in the long run. The alternative to refraining from establishing a budget is experiencing a sense of remorse each time expenditures are made on non-essential items, followed by apprehension regarding the means to cover necessary expenses. In severe instances, the absence of budgeting may result in a precipitous escalation of indebtedness.

Minimal resources are necessary for initiation, in the event that the acquisition of a complimentary electronic document from the internet is unattainable, simply retrieve a notebook and meticulously record your expenses in relation to your income. Are you yet to be persuaded of the significance of implementing a budget? Presented below are additional incentives to drive your determination in establishing and adhering to a carefully planned expenditure framework.

- It is possible to break the cycle of living paycheck to paycheck and establish a savings fund for unforeseen circumstances.

- After creating a budget, the process of alleviating debt is easily attainable.

- Once you have utilized the budget to eliminate your debt, you can employ it to sustain a debt-free status. - Following the utilization of the budget as a means to overcome indebtedness, you can further apply it to maintain a state of financial stability. - Upon successfully employing the budget to alleviate debt, it can subsequently be harnessed to avoid falling back into indebtedness.

Budgeting can aid in eliminating impulsive purchasing behaviors.

Budgeting greatly facilitates the process of saving.

A well-planned financial plan will guarantee uninterrupted utility services since it will always provide sufficient funds for timely payment.

Moreover, effective budgeting will eradicate the anxiety and sleepless nights that stem from fretting over your financial state.

Furthermore, in light of all the aforementioned factors, budgeting will prove to be advantageous in circumstances where one's financial resources are insufficient to accommodate all desired expenditures. It will assist you in restraining excessive expenditure. Moreover, upon the completion of your initial budget formulation and the commencement of its execution, the process of projecting your expenditures and managing your financial resources becomes more streamlined. This can aid you in establishing a plan highlighting the months where financial resources might be limited (Christmas holidays are consistently financially restrictive), allowing for the allocation of additional funds accordingly. A budget will enable you to predict and anticipate the amount of monetary resources that you will have accumulated over a period of six months or one year. With this resource, you have the ability to strategically prepare for a myriad of expenses such as refurbishing your residence, organizing a memorable family excursion, and acquiring a brand-new automobile. Implementing a budget will additionally aid you in your endeavors of long-term financial planning and achieving your goals.

www.ingramcontent.com/pod-product-compliance
Lightning Source LLC
Chambersburg PA
CBHW071701210326
41597CB00017B/2276